For the Sake of Fairytales

poetry & prose
MELISSA M. COMBS

1st Edition

And now these three things remain:
faith, hope, and love.
But the greatest of these is love
- 1 Corinthians 13:13

For the Sake of Fairytales

poetry & prose
MELISSA M. COMBS

FOR THE SAKE OF FAIRYTALES

"But they say if you dream a thing more than once,
it is sure to come true."

-Aurora, *Sleeping Beauty*

FOR THE SAKE OF FAIRYTALES

Dedicated to:

The dreamers — the one's that understand that it is the process of dreaming that is most important, not necessarily the fruition of the dream itself. May you never find yourself too busy, too old, or too cynical to dream. And remember, nothing is final, one must only believe.

FOR THE SAKE OF FAIRYTALES

ONCE UPON A TIME...
IN A KINGDOM FAR, FAR AWAY,
THE HEART OF A PRINCESS
WAS STOLEN.

Some love stories must be rewritten...
if not for the sake of the lovers,
than for the sake of FAIRYTALES.

For the hope of all of humanity,
you and I,
we *mustn't* end this way.

As each and every new stranger
begins to read me
I am reminded how unfortunate
it is that the prologue will always tell of you,
and yet you are nowhere to be found.

How many pages will it take to
revive my soul?
How much ink must I spill
in attempts to wash you away?
Most importantly,
where is this poetic justice
that I hear so much about?

They say that words are powerful,
but I fear that they leave out
what we need to hear the most...
and that is that love knows no other power
but that of it's own.
It is bullet proof, reflecting any and all
streams of words...
and when we are broken-hearted
we have no other choice but to let it
hurt.

I fear to tell the people
that our love was merely momentary,
when they were all as hopeful as I,
God, and the angels.

Knowing that we were born
to be legendary
I must be honest and say
that this separation is
killing me.

And all for what?
A surrender to lust…
to fear…
to complacency?

Yet perhaps still I think
one day
I could be your
Persephone,
and you,
my *Hades.*

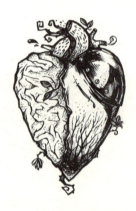

These days it feels as if my DNA
has been altered with instructions
never to forget you…
as if you are here buried deep within my
life's very code.

I am now having a hard time convincing my
limbic system that it has any other responsibilities
outside of preserving thoughts of you.
My blood carries you
and my veins protect and conceal you…
as if I live for you.

Everyone knows that I risked it all for you;
said "even if I am wrong," for you;
gave up a lifetime of religion for you…
yet still I found myself picking up and carrying
my cross, bleeding myself dry for you.

For I so loved this man
that I gave my one and only soul…
that if he shall believe in me
we shall not perish but have eternal life.

A birth,
a death,
and a resurrection,
all for you.

I couldn't pretend and say that I know
myself after meeting you.
Nor could I say that I feel anywhere close
to whole…
not after being broken wide open,
awakened abruptly,
and stripped bare naked
to the bone.

I am now reduced to a cellular level…
rebirthing, unlearning, and learning
about this newfound hunger,
purpose,
and yearning —
all of which is you.

When I am without you
I find myself forfeiting life,
drowning in my sorrows,
and gasping for air until I choke.

When I am with you
only then does my breath return,
the beating of my heart convert,
and the fire inside of my soul burn.

My only question is why must I always die?
For once I wish you had it in you to keep
this heart that beats for you alive.

Is it cursed, this heart of mine?
Instead of rhythmic beats,
it is tachycardia when you are near,
and bradycardia when you are far.

This heart that once belonged to me
now asks for your permission…
it needs to hear you tell it 'fast' or 'slow,'
to heal, to break, or to scar.

I want to know,
where do you run and hide
when thoughts of me project onto
the screen of your mind?
What do you partake in to drown
out the sound?
Who covers your eyes,
afraid of the scenes that you are
bound to revisit or future ones you
will inevitably find?

Who or what distracts you
from the one that best
distracts you?

I refuse to believe that you are truly gone.
Tell me that this is not a forever farewell.
Tell me that this is an
'until I find myself,'
'until I grow,'
'until I see you next time, look into your eyes,
and no longer find it in myself to tell you no.'

This is temporary, right?
Tell me that you could never fully let me go.

When you came into my life
I knew exactly who you were to me.
I saw the cards stacked
against me, so heavily.
I saw the mountain that I was to climb,
and the stakes set
as unforgiving as they were high.

You would be the one to
expand me with your one touch,
and shatter me with the
softest goodbye.

This can't be how the story ends.
You *can't* be Judas,
because as much as I love you…
as good as I am at forgiving…
I am no Jesus.

So come back and tell me that the
thirty pieces is not worth it to you;
that there is no price to what you and I have.
Lie down and sacrifice *for* us,
but please do everything in your power
not to sacrifice us.

I know the storyline.

I'm wise enough to
organize the chapters
and intuitive enough to
guess the final line —
the one that reads,
"when I am strong enough,
I will finally leave."

I know that before
I was born
the plot was formed,
and the details written…
and that if 'strengthen by heartbreak'
were to be spelled out in Morris code,
it would read your name.

But how do I stop loving
the one that I know was sent to
reveal my strength?
The hero disguised as the villain?

I wanted so badly to believe
that you and I were as wild and as
untamable as a firestorm...
but the more time goes on,
the more I fear that we are nothing
more than the embers of cold
and fading sparks.

Yet I keep waiting for the moment that
our now small fire may once more catch wind,
and we could start anew,
as if we had never before seen an end.

So catch hold of me.
Turn our flicker into a flame,
and dance with me until our flame
grows into something timeless and unbroken.

I have found that the problem with
metaphorical blood
is that the drip never ends.
At least if I were to bleed out through my skin
I would pass through hell only to land in peace.
But the way that this heart of mine bleeds for you
leaves me no rest.
I am beautifully tortured, at the very best.

I like to think that if you found me
in a puddle of my own blood
you would finally regret the time lost,
and giving up on our love.
But you don't see it.
You don't see the way that this
invisible wound aches.

I could bleed onto paper,
spew out into your ears,
and still I can't convince you to wake.

Can't you see what this is doing to me?
The way I now favor thoughts of death as opposed
to living this life only half alive?

Everyday I awaken once more only to die.

It is still hard to fathom
that I did in fact hand myself over
entirely to you,
and all for you to decide only to
watch me from afar.
A body that would have bowed to your
every command;
a mind that would have left no room for
the inscription of anyone else's name…
and a heart that would have surrendered
itself to you,
had only you stayed.

I couldn't tell you where he has ran off to,
only what he has left behind…
a woman that would have stood
against all of the world,
wrestled the guard gates of hell,
and even the devil himself
on his behalf;
a woman that would have stood the test of love
against the hands of time.

I couldn't tell you where he is heading to,
only what he has left behind.

And all along
I thought that the intense longing and desire
for you
was as bad as it could possibly get…
but god was I wrong.

Letting go;
telling myself that I had no longer a need for you,
and truly believing it…
that was far worse.

Life faded into the grey, and ever since,
has felt undeniably incomplete.

Let not these writings be in vein
or I may deliver to the world a false hope —
to love, to lose, and to reattain.

Answer when I cry out, my lost love.
Open as I knock.
Give back what you receive of me.

Let us prove to them that true love,
though difficult, is obtainable,
and that two lovers can always be found,
no matter how long they were lost at sea.

Respond to gravities pull this time as it asks
of you to give into me.

Time, all I ask of you is that
as each and every day passes
I recover piece by piece of what this love story
has consequently stolen from me.
It needn't be swift nor miraculous,
only natural —
piece by piece, day by day,
as my undoing too occurred.

Teach me again the magic of everyday,
ordinary things;
remind me of the beauty
that exists outside of him.

What fascination it is to
cut the rays of the sun with a crystal;
to feel the cleansing of the river's water
rush between my toes;
to wake up each and every morning
with no direction,
yet endless possibilities
as to where I should go.

What enchantment it is to live,
to die,
and to live once more,
I yearn to know.

If I can no longer be a part of your reality
then I must become the dream that lingers
every morning long after you wake.
I refuse to be the blur in the background,
or the dream you find yourself
straining to remember.
Remember and revisit me
until I become eerily real to you;
until you ponder
the fulfillment of dreaming verses living.
Lie beneath your sheets and fall into me —
desperately,
deeply,
effortlessly.

How can what's left of you and I
be so much more than fragmented memories?
What took place causing our once blurry scenes
to enliven themselves into crystal clear vibrancy?
I can't help but think that I don't deserve this;
don't want this;
would be better off with fragmentation
over this lucid imagination.

Now I can't seem to shut you out
or peel you off of my mind.
I think of you
until I remember us;
until I waste away hours,
using up every ounce of my time.

But you're not coming back.
You're not losing sleep over the fact
that you're no longer mine.

So depart from me;
spare me;
convince me that of our love
I should resign.

He explains drugs and addiction to me
as if I don't already understand…
as if him leaving this city
wasn't him running off with my supply,
creating an all-powerful feign within me.

I know what I need to know about
dopamine and serotonin.
It's both created by and depleted by him…
a cycle so thrilling
it feels nearly impossible to end.

Where do I find rest,
when you were home to me?
Inspiration, when you were my poetry?
Love... when you were my *one and only*?

I don't know that I ever did truly love myself
until I took pieces of you and
placed them inside of me.

The problem with that though is that
I can no longer choose myself
without choosing you too.

It's like half of everything that I am is you,
and half of everything that
I am after in this life,
because of you...
and if I abandon you now,
I abandon myself too.

You left me in a town beside the ocean
where I swear that the breeze still holds
the ghost of you,
and the salt from the waves,
it tastes just like your skin.

You told me that the big city had plans for you.
Well I pray that it's plans
revealed themselves as faithful and true,
and may the city lights reflect off of your skin
in a way that inspires you.
I pray that as you're walking down the strip,
the music from the bars hit you just right,
and that the nightlife is doing all that it can
to keep you alive.

Know that I will always wish you well,
despite our painful goodbye.

They're different, them and I.
They love with their smiles,
and the glimmers
within their eyes...

I love by grieving memories shared before
mine and your last goodbye.

For every broken hearted soul
there is always an agreement made in despair…
that if one can not live with the one in which
they are madly in love with,
they will desperately settle for their ghost.

'I love you,'
you said,
three times
that night.

And I still haven't
decided if it was
closure,
or salt to my
deepest wound...

to be adored by,
yet never chosen by you.

Willing to die unto myself to revive us,
I face my each and every fear.
Willing to forgive, forget, and forge
new neural-pathways,
I hand myself over to the cause that
is greater than I.
With all that I have;
with all that I am.

But you have yet to show,
and I'm finding it hard now
to believe in the promised land.

Mine and your forever exists inside of me —
a storyline so true that even our circumstances
disagree.

And I doubt, with good reason, that even
death would succeed at taking this truth away from me.

At my last breath
if all for nothing,
then you were my focal point
to ease my troubled mind;
a beautiful memory I will feel
honored to have had the chance to
leave behind.

For love is a privilege,
even if it is not to last.
And I know now that there is no one,
nor thing,
that could ever fully erase
mine and your past.

It was not you and I that
were intended to spontaneously
combust and
fall to the ground.

We were the flames,
meant to burn so brightly that the world
around us inevitably burned itself to ashes.

It was the world that was to burn,
not us.

You know not of what you ask for,
to find in another
everything in which you have ever desired...
there is no freedom in that.

In fact,
it is your very power relinquished;
an enchanting distraction;
your own tailored weakness.

And no longer do you fly freely
but are bound to such attraction,
riddled with fear,
and oftentimes found sleepless.

If losing you taught me anything
I would say that it taught me the ways
of an imposter —
to grit my teeth, force a smile, and to play a roll.

No longer am I human,
no longer this earth my home.
I am an actress —
the ground, my stage;
the script, no longer my own.

When I first thought to write poetry of you,
I had no idea what is was to entail.

Before I could even so much as think to lift
my pen from paper, you had become the main
character of my stories —
a muse as necessary as air.

And there I found you existing
between the bindings
of my books, on every fiber of every page,
and most intimately of all,
in every detail of my being.

I had no idea that you,
my poetry,
were soon to become me.

I love you as if our world
was built upon forgiveness…
breaking bread with you
only to continuously
receive the Judas kiss.

I wonder how long
worldly pleasures can fulfill a man
once he has had a taste of true love.
And too I wonder when you will find it in you
to turn your back against the priests,
and declare you and I,
once and for all,
enough.

I wish people knew the truth
about selling one's soul.

It's like they always tell you,
the devil is not red with pointed horns,
but rather he is every detail of
your most intimate desires.

Such as this,
there is no visible contract;
no sign on the dotted line.

It is meeting and then losing
the love of your life.

It is having nothing left but
a wide open, and vulnerable soul.

You put your pen to paper and eventually...
you sell it —
in hopes of reaching the others like you;
in hopes or releasing even just
an ounce of the pain;
in hopes of loosening up it's hold.
But either way you spin it...
it is your soul, on paper...
and soon enough,
it
is
sold.

At this point
I don't see how either
one of us could be proud
of ourselves.
We took a love,
sacred and rare,
and we left it to
fade into the ruins.
All that is left of us now
is surface level lust
and idle promises
made in despair.

And sometimes we both look
up to the heavens for one another,
but deep down we both know
we can no longer be found there.

I would take a dagger to the heart;
Juliet my way back to you,
and still you would ask
the god of the underworld
to take you away from me...
allowing lust once more to fill your cup.

For once,
I just wish that our love was enough.

What I remember most of that night with you
was the electricity shared between us;
the frequency in which we shone.

And of the deep water that we found ourselves in,
I made note…
lovers of falsity
dare not to stand a chance,
rather they would drown.

But you and I,
when wet,
we sparked like never before.

That's when I finally understood our love —
that we loved in alternating currents, voltage,
and magnetism, but never in the stabilized love
needed to survive in this world.

I don't know if it's pitiful or if it's admirable,
but I thought maybe, just maybe,
if I vowed my love fully indestructible
for you;
crossed myself over for you,
and even turned myself inside out for you,
soon you would ache never again to leave my side.

It was myself against the most unforgiving elements;
against each and every odd...
always something new, that in your name,
I must face.

What love this is —
love that in which I have never before known;
where an insatiable hunger and a stubborn
determination collide.
I'd give up my hardest sins for our love to survive.

My lover hides from me.
It is an inborn instinct,
submerging himself in the dark,
as he lies in wait.

Meanwhile
I awaken inside of me the strength
required to become his prey.

Soon there are sunken in teeth,
bloodstained clothes,
and curled toes.

Never in a million years would I have
foreseen myself giving into a man
as such, for his childish ways.

But love, I have learned
makes little sense, if ever any at all…
and for the ones that we love,
we open ourselves wide,
bare our chests,
and embrace the fall.

Man or monster
I can hardly tell…
nor can I decipher if your
never ending returns are cruel
or kind.

By nightfall I could swear that we
are ill-omened,
but come morning
I can always be found praising
all things holy.

Could it be that our love
is forever doomed a
world of the in-between?

I say if only you would open your eyes,
I could take you to places heavenly.
You say, if only I could surrender mine,
you could take me somewhere
transcendent of time.

But until then,
you and I both know
we are earthly;
bound;
confined.

I have lost him to
his fear,
to his lusts,
to his second guessing…
but above all,
to time.

Therefore
I am convinced,
and beyond the ability
to be swayed…
this world has little mercy
for hearts as mine.

If I must accept you leaving, I will…
but please don't leave me inside of our last memory.
Come back and let us end what we so long ago
began…
this time softly;
sweetly.

It is no secret that when it comes to you
I will always be found weak.
When I hear your name, even years later,
I still find myself buckling at the knees.
I tell myself I would cross oceans,
move mountains, and wrestle fate for you.

Why not barter with the devil for you,
split myself in two, descend to hell,
bleed myself dry, if you asked me to?

I hate the days that I allot myself too much time.
Too much time and I find myself thinking —
thinking and I find myself crashing back into you —
crashing back into you and I lose myself all over again —
lose myself and I am in need of saving…

and you and I both know, you are no savior…
at least not for me.

I only knew how to love in metaphors.

You only knew how to love like the tide…
crashing into me, only to pull away.

Cursed are these lungs that breathe for you;
cursed is this heart that beats for you;
this mind that sifts through our memories,
and relentlessly dreams up future scenes.

There is no blessing for a heart that loves
what is incapable of loving it back.

Though our story has ended
it will not stop us from re-reading
one another
a thousand times,
and a thousand times over again.
After all,
ink has sacrificially spilled
in order to create us,
corners of pages have bent
in desperation to preserve us,
and bindings of books have
martyred themselves to carry us through
the hands of time.

Open me up once more.
Place me upon your lips.
Forever embed me into your mind.

You bring out the very best in me;
you bring out the absolute worst in me.

Today my thirst is quenched
only tomorrow to find that
I am bloodthirsty.
My fingers caress your heart
until my hands wrap their way
around your neck.

My heart and my mind have lost
their sync,
and I blame it all on the day
that you left.

If ever Adam wished a leveling
revenge upon Eve,
I imagine his wish fulfilled
when you told me you loved me,
only to up and leave.

Now I'm wishing that I were crueler;
wishing I would have had you
bite the apple for me;
wishing I would have
commanded the serpent to
circle your neck,
and hang you from Eden's tree.

I should have lived out a reason
for your revenge upon thee.

I hope to forget you in the next life.
I hope the next life to be fair, rather than cruel.
I hope that when the angels ask you to sign
the contract,
you wish to refuse too.

I hope by then the separation travels
further than my bones,
crash lands into my DNA,
and splits my double helix in two.

I hope by then I am finally rid of you.

Why if I were born to write stories
must the one of you and I die?
I find it too hard of a task to tug and
pull at the words simply to carry them through.
So I refuse to write of future fairytales
unless the one of you and I is to finally come true.
This is the only story I have ever cared enough
to write.

These are more than words,
but a living, breathing soul, putting up
it's best fight.

I never did run with the intentions of hiding.
It was something of nature
that inevitably kicked in.
A protective barrier maybe?
A defense mechanism.

I know one thing
with absolute certainty though…
it had nothing to do with me
not loving you.

I loved you to a calibre that was unmatched.
Because notice,
as soon as I left you,
I had no other choice but
to come crawling right back.

I dare them to tell me that my love for you
was anything other than brave.

I might as well have stood naked, baring my skin
for all of the world, while being burned at the stake.

That's what these words are after all —
a soul, stripped.
And though I face the world shaking, vulnerably…
still I face it.

'Too far gone,'
that's what they all say.
But I picked the locks to the gates of hell
to escape this pain.
I bled for this;
exposed my heart for this;
gave up too much of myself to accept loss,
and no gain.

I can't leave you now.

And just when I am confident that your pull
has released me with a final act of mercy,
gravity fails me yet again.

I'm not sure what the future holds for me,
but if I am honoring my current truths,
I'd say that time is a liar and hope, a thief…
and that not a day goes by that I don't wish
that you were right here next to me.

I didn't dodge all of your bullets
to now slip off my clothing for you,
baring nude my chest.

When I think of my chest
and you, same sentence…
I think of the cruelness of how you
never did check in on it.

What was the rhythm to my heart
following the years that you left;
the weight, the emptiness, the heaviness?

I'll tell you,
brokenness.

If I would have known
that they were coming for us
soon after we met,
I swear I would have
loved you better than I did.

My heart went to war
the day that you left.
Years later I have yet
to surrender these weapons…
for any proposal,
any case,
or any cause.

I am forever enlisted,
and I will always fight for you.

If I can survive
this kind of heartache,
surely when the day comes,
I will master death.

There was a darkness to him,
but god was there so much light.

And had I not seen it within him,
perhaps by now I would have found it in me
the strength to let him go.

But how do you tell the heart,
an organ that was built to withstand
all of hell,
to give up such a meaningful fight?

How, and more than that, why?

Every time I think to throw the towel in,
there it is again…
his light.

I have tried desperately to land often
on thoughts other than you.
I think of what it would be like to land
on the moon,
but then my mind travels right back to
thoughts of landing onto you.

I think of the ocean
and all of its vastness,
but then it reminds me that your mind
is much like its depths,
and in that simple thought alone
it erects
emotions that I find nearly impossible to check.

I think of open fields and the wild flowers
they tend to hold,
but it only reminds me of how I once
wished to grow into you
so wildly…
without any rhyme or reason…
how I wished to root into you and
weather any storm and season.

I have tried so desperately to land on thoughts
other than you…
but I can never seem to find a good enough reason.

They tell me that you don't deserve this —
all of these tears disguising themselves
as Times New Romans.
And god do I wish that's
what you believed this all was…
nothing more than font, than ink, than art…
not the physical fatality of this once whole,
yet now abandoned,
and incomplete heart.

"Write of someone new.
He never has, nor never will deserve you."
But they are nothing more than outsiders
observing pieces to a story.
[obscure and incomplete views]
You are half of me now;
I am half of you.
Though perfectly imperfect,
blended,
broken,
and bruised…

we are one now;
no longer are we wandering this earth
as two.

You left us somewhere forgettable;
somewhere unworthy of even mentioning…
and I found that I just couldn't accept that.
So I set off for Salem,
in search of something more —
myself.

And there I found her,
burning, in agony, yet rising, at the stake…
as all that was left of you and her was
finally set ablaze.

They say power tastes better than love,
and hell, after my evolution, I'd have to say
that maybe it does…
but the cruelest part, is that even still,
I would have chosen us.

Forgive me,
I was under the impression
that you and I were both
moved first by spirit,
then by flesh.

But nevertheless,
if flesh is to overpower,
why am I not your chosen sin?
Who is it that you are choosing
to undress?

You tell me that you will
always come back to me and that
one day you will marry me.
But I wonder if you notice
how often lust trips you up.

I wish you understood that we will not live forever,
and that there is only so much time left
for us.

I wish you would ask
for forgiveness,
repent,
and choose love.

Somewhere in this god forsaken world
there must exist a map to your soul —
one that would lead me back to you...
the real you; the you that
I caught a glimpse of so long ago.

To the rest of the world
I wouldn't mind becoming a ghost.
I haven't a good reason as to why I would need
any of them to remember my name.

But when it comes to you,
I am terrified of one day being forgotten.
Please let our love not be in vein.

These days
I dream of you less,
think of you less...
and I wouldn't dare
ask that you be sent
back to me.

I've worked hard to get
to where I am today.

I picked myself up,
brushed myself off,
and developed thicker skin.

But this poem is a lie,
and I would do it all over again.

Everyday is nearly the same story for me.
I tell myself today is the day that I will stop
connecting our memories to every love song
I hear on the radio,
and today I will stop thinking of you...
obsessively, at least.

I will become the high priestess that everyone
speaks of, place you back where it was that
I first found you,
and I will reach for my dignity instead.

Today will be the day that I get you out of my head...
but if not today, then maybe when I am dead.

It's ironic isn't it?
That you were the one
that taught me never to look
back, only ahead...

and yet it's felt nearly impossible
ever since you left.

Your silence is a blood curling scream..
so why must your words be what enlivens me?
I'm sure my mother and father wished for me
to love something; someone; anything
that loved me back in consistency…
but you have never been the one to give that to me.
I think you love me in theory;
I think when you feel me slip from reach
your skin crawls itself off of it's bones
to tell me it's sorry.

But what about when I am before you?
When we have everything and yet nothing
to prove?
What about then,
when I submit myself to you?

The pressure is off,
no elemental surprises;
not a reason in the world to be afraid?

Why won't you love me then?

Sometimes I think back to the
day that we first met.
I imagine what it would have been like
to walk into that bar, and see you sitting there,
just as you once did.
Only this time
I would find a table close by,
your back still turned to me…
and I would sit and
I would just silently observe for
a moment instead.

I would take a sip of my water,
wipe a tear from eye,
and tell myself that
though it looked promising enough,
you were never going to let me keep you…
not fully at least.

I would give myself a few moments to grieve…
and just when you would begin to check the time,
worried about me…
I would take a deep breath, close my tab,
and I would leave.

All I ever wanted was to melt your heart;
to seep onto the ice like warm honey...
until the numbness was no more;
until the cruelness of this world was no more;
until you finally knew the true sweetness of warmth.

How in the hell did I, in turn,
let you drive me so far away?

Your coldness repelled me
until my own heart went numb;
until I finally understood the cruelness of this world,
until there was no warmth or sweetness,
only a bitter chill.

The irony is almost funny —
a cold romance
both beginning
and ending in the months of summer.

Sadly
I am everything I envisioned myself being
without you.
Ironically, in that everything,
there is a noticeable nothing.

There is a weight that is crushing,
and a void that threatens to wipe me clean.
I can feel it most days
crawling it's way down my spine,
landing itself first into my heart,
and next, into my spleen.

But still in the midst of the unrest
I have yet to decide if this
is a nightmare, or a dream?
To love and to lose;
to know that there was once a me
that existed alongside you.

My serotonin has seemed to increase.
It's seeping out,
and mixing with his.
It's messing with my equilibrium…
and I don't know what to think of this.
In it's peak
is where I wish to keep it,
but now that he is gone,
I am hopelessly depleted.

Time is not linear,
not in the sense that I once believed.
It can't be.

Though change is inevitable,
and the seasons arrive
so that we may shed our skin…
our change is rarely ever a destination,
but merely fleeting moments passing by.

And this…
this is neither good nor bad,
meaning it is neither our final hello,
nor our final goodbye.

When the angel of death
comes for me
he'll be disappointed to learn
that you came for me long ago…
that I have been dead inside
ever since you left.

There is a me that exists
even after crashing into you…
I have to believe that.

Somewhere out there
she is her own person again.
Her identity isn't this pitiful
showcasing of memories
of who she was when she was with you.

So many impressive words
just to say…

I needed you

and,

where were you?

I've lost a lot to paranoia,
though none of it measurable
compared to losing you.

I think I dreamt up
that you were out to get me.
I think I dreamt up
that I wasn't good enough for you.
I think I dreamt up
that I'd lose you.

Until you were…
until I wasn't…
until I did.

But if you came back to me
I swear I would find my self worth,
if it meant finally letting you in.

It's mid July
and I am asked
"why the chills?"

Because it was winter
when I first felt the warmth of his
blood coursing his veins,
penetrating through each and
every layer of my skin...
and summer when he left...
that's when the frost bite set in.

I know you question it too…
worlds apart
and you ask yourself
how two souls,
now exist so effortlessly as one…
beyond the distance,
beyond the faults,
even beyond the written expectations
of two souls that have harmed one another.

You and I,
we are the exception.

All of this time
I blamed you for leaving me,
but now I see…
it is the others that have left;
that may always leave.

But you are here
to protect me from it all.

In my mind
I am free to always
travel back to you.
In my heart,
you and I exist indefinitely.

I am sorry that I ran from you,
but if I am being honest,
I am sorry just as much
for running back to you.

If I could change anything
I would have let us die slow…
not this quick intensity of
crash landing into a burn.
I would have savored us,
released you, and returned to myself
in a reasonable flow.

Maybe we weren't indestructible,
you and I…
maybe all along it was only you that was.

So I loved you with a ferocity
that was too much for you.

At the end of it all,
I loved you without fear…
and I could *never* regret that.

We were somewhere between toxic and iconic;
between we wanted our fix,
yet no longer were we willing to buy it.　`

The comedown became a little more evident,
getting high lost it's relevance….
and though we swore we never could
I think we both began to regret it.

Our addiction covered up as love,
that's all it ever was…
and we were finally able to admit it.

Our time has come
and we are nothing more than a crime scene.
If you watch and listen for the angels
they are wiping up our blood as they
convince the onlookers that
there is nothing left to see.

We didn't pass away peacefully.
We struggled, and squirmed,
taking our last breath violently.

I have nothing left for you;
you have nothing left for me.

This is more than a goodbye I fear,
this is a final 'Rest in Peace'

Maybe there is a tragedy in holding
too much of the light,
just as there is in holding
too much of the dark.
I like to think that's why you and I met —
a transference of energy;
an instilling of balance.
And maybe that is all that you and I
were ever meant for...
to merge, and then to part
into something new.

When the wine touches my tongue
I try not to think of you,
but when it hits my stomach;
my mind;
my soul…
I have no other choice.
It trickles down my throat,
and my thoughts bleed Truth.
You are anywhere and everywhere to me,
like an omnipresent God to
mere human.

I need you,
but don't you dare forget that you need
me too.
What is a god without worship?
An alter void of knees?
A creator without his creation?
You without me?

Truth be told,
I don't care who you lie with
or even who you lie to,
only that you stop lying to yourself.

We should have followed the theme of
the classic fairytales; we should have
not only endured the weapons formed against
us but conquered them.

What distracted you?
Was it worth it?
Are you happy?

FOR THE SAKE OF FAIRYTALES...
let your guard down,
and tell me that you miss me.

One of the hardest things
I have had to accept is that
maybe you are a knight in shining armor…
you just aren't mine.
And maybe you really are a good man…
just not to me.
Maybe you are stepping more and more
into honor, valor, and righteousness everyday.
But I was left behind,
you are just simply too far gone,
and the progress was never meant for me to see.

If ever you look back on us
I pray you find it in you
to peer past all of the mistakes
that you and I both made…
all of the carelessness,
and all of the pain.

May all that's left be the truth and
only the truth —
that you and I were simply
two people, who were afraid of love…
yet despite it all,
damnit did we try.

All I ever wanted was to create something
with you that was cinematic,
but I think that's where I lost you —
when you realized that I had a flare for theatrics.
And listen,
I don't mean to come across as dramatic,
but what is life if not a stage,
and what are moments if not sacred?
Where do we begin and end, if not a script?
This could be our very last moment...

WAIT!
this is it...

THIS

IS

IT!

yet despite the heartache,
STILL SHE FOUND HER
HAPPILY EVER AFTER

Pick up your pen and rewrite your fairytale.

Sleeping beauty can and will awaken sooner,
Cinderella doesn't have to be enslaved for as long,
and Rapunzel defeats the witch at the first sign of
distress.

You are a queen,
and you deserve every ounce of this.

What is this?
Where am I?
This midway point
between mourning a lost love,
and worshipping all that is new…

between losing him,
and loving you.

Everyday I have to remind myself
that you are not him.
You are in fact where mine and his
story ends,
and where my belief
in true love is meant to begin.

You speak into the silence that he left behind;
you kiss the open wounds
he once created and refused to bind.
Therefore, I will allow you within,
as I release him once and for all
from this heart of mine.

If I would have known
that God had a plan
to bring you into my life,
I would have never wasted
a single moment
peering into my past.
I would have boldly and eagerly
left what was never mine long behind.

After him
I could feel myself growing weary.
All of the sorrow and the heaviness
sent my soul into the deepest sleep.

But when you kissed me,
I awakened from life as sleeping beauty.

I could have never
planned for you
because I was too distracted
with someone who refused
to plan with me.

You are my happiest accident;
my *serendipity.*

If you're going to love me,
you will have to love me through my
fear for a while longer.
Override my conditioning of believing
that love is simply a word —
an order that mere humans could
never possibly live up to…
and then live up to it,
until I believe.

Love is new for me.

I think if two people have a hard time
letting go of one another,
they never truly will.
Though their bodies may part,
they will cling to one another,
via their soul,
their mind,
and their heart.

You are dimensional travel —
something beyond the bleakness
I have since infancy known of this world.

You are my souls recognition;
my northern star;
my one and only compass back *home.*

To love something;
someone, so deeply,
I knew that
there were only
two choices before me:
to carefully and meticulously
guard my heart,
or to love with a wildness
that said no matter
the height from which I may fall,
nor the impact of the crash,
I would not let it stop me from
diving in.

I have always and will always
love you with that wildness.

A woman sincerely in love
becomes these two things
I am sure of...
both *enchanted*,
and *poetic*.

The truth is,
I love you as the embodiment of your
entire family lineage plus more.
I am the mother that you wish
would have chosen you over all of those men.
I am the father that would have done things
differently this go round,
taking your hand and guiding you from a fearful
young boy into a secure and confident man.
I am the grandparents that would have done away
with their bad habits to simply
buy more time with you;
the sibling that you looked up to, yet who's eyes
were nowhere to be found…
mine would have found yours; *they have.*

I am more than a lover,
I am a lover who's soul has been set on fire…
and I will burn for you until
I see that child that died inside of you rebirth
with a new and fair chance at life.

Unlike a hunger
I did not form my love
for you through famish.
It was not a thrill,
a high, or a chase.
It was simply loving
what was before me,
and so desperately
wishing for it to stay.

Lead me into the darkness
like a sheep to slaughter
and then save me from the fate
of the flock.

For then, and only then
will I trust that I am more than mere
flesh to you.

Prove to me that your love for me
is prioritized
over your hunger or thirst for me,
and only then may you devour me,
having all of me —
body, mind, and soul.

They say it's not love, it's attachment,
and I respond "then to hell with love."

They say it's attachment because of my
trauma, and I say
"well thank god for trauma then."

~~They say~~
I say
it's less about any of that than it is about him.
It is only him and has always been him.

I care less about coining a word
to match the way
that I feel
than I do about how I actually,
in my bones,
and to my very core feel.

I need no other evidence to build my case,
no word;
no explanation;
only him.

If I am being honest,
I think I have only ever loved what was
unfathomably out of reach…
until you.

With you I love so dearly what is right before me.

Must everything and everyone
be let go of?

In the hands of the world I am but
a baby,
given, only to be taken from.

Bur I never knew just how okay
I was with this preexisting law
until the day that I met you.

'Cruel' was my first thought;
'stand and fight', my very next.

Suddenly I forgot the way of surrender,
and channeled my inner Athena instead.

I will fight for you.
I will die for you.
I will, come hell or high waters
lie for you.

But never will I lie down as they take
you away from me.
I am tried and tested, through and through,
in relentless pursuit of you.

We are where the myth first begins,
discretely masquerading in the clothing
of an ordinary love story…
but you and I both know that there is nothing
even remotely close to ordinary between us.

One day they will write stories of us —
immeasurable desire,
fear, longing, pain — crystalized.
What we once believed to be a fleeting moment
in time, immortalized.

I know that I can get a little dramatic
over you and I,
as if I am acting…
but I can promise you
there is no script clever enough
that I could write,
nor any stage large enough
that I could stand on
that would fully convey
my love for you.

The evolution of my love
could never be predicted.
There is no director, no cast,
no camera…
this is raw, and honest,
and entirely unscripted.

Of all of the poetry that I have ever read,
all of the legends that I have ever been told,
and all of the romance films I have ever seen,
I realize, you are exactly that, for me…
a story so alluring
that the natural world would always find it
impossible to believe.

How could I ever feel anything
other than love for you?
Before I even fully knew myself in this life,
it was you that first inspired me.
Once but a stranger,
only to become the other half of me.
Void of words,
of art,
of magic,
and suddenly you became my poetry.

If I were to begin drowning
in the depths of you
I am certain I would only dive deeper.
There would no longer be an option
other than sink or swim for me.
And if I were in fact to sink…
I would breathe in the water until
I had taken up residence in the sea.

I would do whatever it takes,
be whoever I needed to be,
just to keep you here next to me.

I was in favor of absolutes;
something tangible.
I had everything in my life
perfectly planned
and laid out accordingly
(of which he was not included.)

But men like him,
with their dangerous and
nomadic nature,
they have a way of challenging
your innermost thoughts and feelings.

And no longer did I need safety,
but freedom,
and possibilities.

And no longer was I a soul
of the sedentary,
but of the gypsy.

All I ask is that on
the ordinary days
you remember all that is
extraordinary between us.
On the hard days,
you stick around until night fall,
and you sink into me,
easily.

Life is cruel,
but you and I,
we don't have to be.

When I was a child
I was so fascinated with
antonyms, synonyms,
and metaphors.

It all makes sense to me now —
being in love with you;
needing access to the entire
english dictionary
and it still feeling as though it is not
enough for me to describe my love for you.

It will start as this…
a few simple words;
a poem here and there;
a chapter;
a book.

I will introduce him softly,
slowly,
subtly…
until ultimately he exists
upon every new page.

He gave to me my fairytale life,
therefore I will write him into his.

The way that you love me is more than
a retribution for my past lover's sins against me.

We are larger than our bodies
I note,
as you
exit yours,
entering mine.

We are freer than
this heavy marrow.

See
if the hydrogen,
nitrogen,
carbon,
and oxygen
were to be
obliterated,
all that is left
is you...
that is me —
a complexity learning such simplicity.

May each and every
word that falls from my lips
form sentences
in hopes to
lie with you,
not to you;
lie down and await you,
not lie you down to
obliterate you.

May they form a fortress
where your soul may
find it's sweetest
rest.

I think often of the way
that it bothered most men
when I told them that I
wasn't looking for love,
but an endless game;
the way that their smiles
fled instantaneously
from their faces.
Hearts were broken
before even fully opening,
and towels were thrown in
somewhere around the space
that I intended their bodies to lay.
I never understood much of their fear,
their reasoning for choosing not to play.

But when I saw you…
when I gazed into your eyes
and sensed your willingness to stay…
your fearlessness became the atonement
for their weaknesses,
and your competitive nature,
the
end
of
the
game.

I close my eyes and I can be anything
I want to be in this world…
and still I choose only to be yours.

I know this of my mind so far…
it is a masterful creator —
capable of knitting together
the most intricate of details,
from any timeline, era,
culture, or fantasy
one could ever think of.

Yet still in all of it's vastness
it tends to favor thoughts of you.

If ever your soul
is taken off to war
I would transfer my soul's
very own peace
to ensure come nightfall
you collected your sleep.

Your wounds are my wounds,
your fight, my very own,
and I would always
cover the front line
if it meant a prompt
and safe return home.

With you
I feel like a young child again.
I look to the sky,
and the rays of the sun,
they finally bend and break again.
There is a kaleidoscope of colors
that I had long forgotten.
Again, nature speaks to me,
and wonder enchants me —

who I could be;
who *we* could be,
is suddenly infinite.

There is enough persuasion in the way
that you and I bleed for one another
to move the entire heavens into supporting
us, should we wish for it to.
We could conquer cities,
unravel century old mysteries;
carve the names of ourselves
and our entire lineages into history.

I always wondered what it would feel like
to float in zero gravity.
It has to be this; *belonging to you* —
where all of life feels effortless,
and the heaviness that I feared
would never leave finally dissipates…
where all of the acceleration forces
upon me finally add to zero
by the mere touch of your skin.

Let us show them
that everlasting love is not a gift,
but a decision.
Let us offer unto one another
grace,
forgiveness,
and a willingness to survive
all that the world may throw
against us.

I choose love over lust.
Daily, I choose you.
Forever, I choose us.

In all of this worlds vastness
it really is something
when two souls come together
and decide that one another
is more than enough.

I have the heart of a mermaid,
and you have the depth of the sea.

As fate would tell us,
some love stories are simply meant to be.

I need you to know this…
what you and I have is all that
I have ever dreamt of.
Yes, there were others before you,
and yes, I felt something for them,
but it could never compare to this…
the love that you and I share.

You took my love and
you reciprocated it.
You took the light inside of my soul
and you magnified it…
and you took the cynicism
that I once carried,
and you destroyed it.

I now see no other,
desire no other,
need no other…
only you.

On the outside
sometimes I may appear to be
so ordinarily in love with you…
but inwardly I am as a child
splashing in a puddle for the first time;
I am as a moth compelled to fly into the flame;
a poet's love and obsession for rhymes…
I am exceptionally in love,
dancing and squealing,
until I lose sight of all of reality,
and all of time.

When did I know that I was in love with you?
When I sat down without a thing in this world to
distract me
and my thoughts of you manifested into a
physical feeling so profound that I could have
sworn you had reached out and touched me,
yet you were no where to be found…

that had to have been when.

It is true that the light is within us
and that we need nothing outside of ourselves...
I really do believe this.
But I'd be lying if I said
I didn't notice that my soul
went from a mere glimmer
to the light of the entire world,
set on fire,
the day that I found you.

This time I'll do it right.
I'll love the one that loves me…
and I will love him
profusely;
irrevocably;
unconditionally.

If you will allow it
I have come so that I may do more than
brim mere surface.
I want to know what it feels like when wet,
and above all, what lies beneath.
I want to first float,
and then to sink.
I want all of your depth inviting,
surrounding, and consuming me.

And never mind the need to breathe…
I'll leave that for those that choose to dwell on land.
I have come so that your ocean may have me,
and I have left behind my fear of disintegrating
into the shore's sand.

My need for you is and always will be
far more compelling than my
need for an easy and safe place to land.

My love,
they were chapters
and they were fleeting.
You are books,
to me — an entire series.

I think it only happens
once in a lifetime.
I think you feel it
for only that one person…
that moment of complete
and total surrender, you know?
Where suddenly the world stops spinning
just long enough
to whisper to you.
It's a faint whisper, but god is it vivid…
that no matter
the fate of you two,
whether you crash or burn;
sink or swim…
their love will forever change you.

I refuse to miss out on mine
and your fairytale
by reminiscing any longer
on previous nightmares,
once disguised as love.

Sometimes after the wreckage
I guess we really do find our safe harbor...
mine is *you*.

Everywhere I turn there are songs
singing of lost love,
poems with reminiscent themes,
and the focus on what
could have been.
Rarely is it appreciation
of the here and the now...
stories like the one of you and I.
Lets change that.

If they knew what it was like
to face the unknown
of everyday only to sink into the
soft and secure known
of what is waiting for them back home,
I think they would shift their focus from
what could have been to what is;
what fought to survive;
what endures any and everything
to stay alive —
much like the story of you and I.

I understand it all
as clear as day now.
I was no wondrous.
I wasn't this wild,
unsatisfied, and untamable
gypsy that I had been led to believe.

Because now that
I have found you…
my longing,
my restlessness,
my roaming…
it's all ceased.

I hope it happens for you.
That one day you just wake up
and you finally believe good things for yourself.
You decide that you deserve the fairytale
and you walk away from the
seductive, yet destructive nightmare.
I hope more than this
that you find it in you to set fire to it,
as you walk away…
and that as it all dissipates,
catching into a thousand flames,
may you never once look back.

I hope you run headlong
into your happily ever after.

There is a great lesson of 'Beauty and the Beast,' that a thing must be loved before it is lovable.

- G.K Chesterson

ACKNOWLEDGEMENTS

My readers, experiencing my work through each and every one of your perceptions is nothing short of magical to me. I cherish hearing from all of you, and I thank you endlessly for supporting my work.

My children, though I may have found motivation in this world outside of you... none of it is measurable in comparison to the way that you motivate me. Thank you for giving me such great purpose, outside of myself.

My parents, for the consistent encouragement and belief in me, and for helping me every step of the way.

Stef, for being the set of wings that have helped carry me through this journey in real life, before it ever formed itself into words.

Monroe, for choosing me and for showing me kindness, love, patience, and support... of which we all yearn to receive in this life.

FOR THE SAKE OF FAIRYTALES

With all of my love,
MELISSA M. COMBS

The Enchanted Poetess

Instagram: @theenchantedpoetess
Tiktok: @theenchantedpoetess_

Made in the USA
Las Vegas, NV
10 December 2023

82461908R00114